THE
christmas
cook

p

This is a Parragon Book
This edition published in 2006

Parragon
Queen Street House
4 Queen Street
Bath BA1 1HE, UK

ISBN: 1-40548-028-9

Printed in China

Cover design by Shelley Doyle-20 Twenty Design

This edition design by Clare Barber
Text by the Bridgewater Book Company
Photography by Mark Wood
Home Economist Pamela Gwyther

notes for the reader

- This book uses both metric and imperial measurements. Follow the same units of measurement throughout; do not mix metric and imperial.
- All spoon measurements are level: teaspoons are assumed to be 5 ml, and tablespoons are assumed to be 15 ml.
- Unless otherwise stated, milk is assumed to be full fat, eggs and individual vegetables such as potatoes are medium, and pepper is freshly ground black pepper.
- Recipes using raw or very lightly cooked eggs should be avoided by infants, the elderly, pregnant women, convalescents and anyone suffering from an illness.
- Optional ingredients, variations or serving suggestions have not been included in the calculations.
- The times given are an approximate guide only. Preparation times differ according to the techniques used by different people and the cooking times may also vary.

contents

introduction

Enjoying delicious food is an intrinsic part of Christmas. Where would we be without the seasonal delights of succulent turkey and cranberries, sweet mince pies and rich Christmas pudding? And who could imagine the festivities without the party cheer of Hot Rum punch and the sweet spices of mulled wine?

This book features a dazzling array of festive recipes that will conjure up the cheer of the season wherever you happen to be. You'll find many traditional favourites here, such as roast turkey, Christmas pudding, mince pies and a sherry trifle. There are also contemporary and international dishes, such as Sliced Duck Breast with Madeira & Blueberries and Mozzarella Crostini with Pesto & Caviar. Vegetarians will enjoy the Feta Cheese & Cranberry Tarts and the Mixed Nut Roast with Cranberry & Red Wine Sauce.

Christmas is a time for truly mouthwatering fare, whether you are entertaining a large group of people or curling up with home-made treats in front of a crackling fire. So, wherever you will be this Christmas, and whatever you are planning to do, there will be something here to suit the occasion.

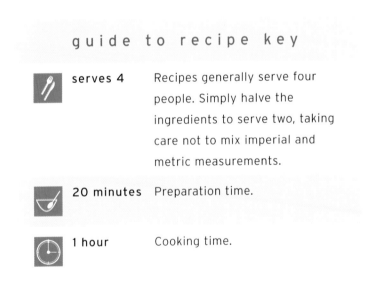

guide to recipe key

serves 4 — Recipes generally serve four people. Simply halve the ingredients to serve two, taking care not to mix imperial and metric measurements.

20 minutes — Preparation time.

1 hour — Cooking time.

soups & starters

turkey, leek & stilton soup

 serves 4   15 minutes   25 minutes

ingredients

4 tbsp butter

1 large onion, chopped

1 leek, trimmed and sliced

325 g/11$\frac{1}{2}$ oz cooked turkey
   meat, sliced

600 ml/1 pint chicken stock

150 g/5$\frac{1}{2}$ oz Stilton cheese

150 ml/5 fl oz double cream

1 tbsp chopped fresh tarragon

pepper

fresh tarragon leaves and croûtons,
   to garnish

method

- Melt the butter in a saucepan over a medium heat. Add the onion and cook, stirring, for 4 minutes, until slightly softened. Add the leek and cook for another 3 minutes.

- Add the turkey to the pan and pour in the stock. Bring to the boil, then reduce the heat and simmer gently, stirring occasionally, for about 15 minutes. Remove from the heat and leave to cool a little.

- Transfer half of the soup into a food processor and blend until smooth. Return the mixture to the pan with the rest of the soup, stir in the Stilton, cream and tarragon and season with pepper. Reheat gently, stirring. Remove from the heat, pour into 4 warm soup bowls, garnish with tarragon and croûtons and serve.

wild mushroom & sherry soup

 serves 4   15 minutes   35 minutes

ingredients

2 tbsp olive oil

1 onion, chopped

1 garlic clove, chopped

125 g/4½ oz sweet potato, peeled
    and chopped

1 leek, trimmed and sliced

200 g/7 oz white and chestnut
    mushrooms

150 g/5½ oz mixed wild mushrooms

600 ml/1 pint vegetable stock

350 ml/12 fl oz single cream

4 tbsp sherry

salt and pepper

Parmesan shavings and sautéed wild
    mushrooms, sliced, to garnish

method

- Heat the oil in a saucepan over a medium heat. Add the onion and garlic and cook, stirring, for 3 minutes until softened slightly. Add the sweet potato and cook for another 3 minutes. Stir in the leek and cook for another 2 minutes.

- Stir in the mushrooms, stock and cream. Bring to the boil, then reduce the heat and simmer gently, stirring occasionally, for about 25 minutes. Remove from the heat, stir in the sherry, and leave to cool a little.

- Transfer half of the soup into a food processor and blend until smooth. Return the mixture to the pan with the rest of the soup, season with salt and pepper and reheat gently, stirring. Pour into 4 warm soup bowls, and garnish with Parmesan shavings and wild mushrooms.

spiced pumpkin soup

 serves 4   15 minutes   35 minutes

ingredients

2 tbsp olive oil

1 onion, chopped

1 garlic clove, chopped

1 tbsp chopped fresh root ginger

1 small red chilli, deseeded and
    finely chopped

2 tbsp chopped fresh coriander

1 bay leaf

1 kg/2 lb 4 oz pumpkin, peeled, deseeded
    and diced

600 ml/1 pint vegetable stock

salt and pepper

single cream, to garnish

method

- Heat the oil in a saucepan over a medium heat. Add the onion and garlic and cook, stirring, for about 4 minutes, until slightly softened. Add the ginger, chilli, coriander, bay leaf and pumpkin and cook for another 3 minutes.

- Pour in the stock and bring to the boil. Using a slotted spoon, skim any scum from the surface. Reduce the heat and simmer gently, stirring occasionally, for about 25 minutes, or until the pumpkin is tender. Remove from the heat, take out the bay leaf and leave to cool a little.

- Transfer the soup into a food processor and blend until smooth (you may have to do this in batches). Return the mixture to the pan and season with salt and pepper. Reheat gently, stirring. Remove from the heat, pour into 4 warm soup bowls, garnish each one with a swirl of cream and serve.

mozzarella crostini
with pesto & caviar

 serves 4   20 minutes   15 minutes

ingredients

8 slices white bread, crusts removed

3 tbsp olive oil

200 g/7 oz mozzarella, cut into
     thin pieces

6 tbsp lumpfish caviar

PESTO

75 g/2³⁄₄ oz fresh basil, finely chopped

35 g/1¹⁄₄ oz pine kernels, finely chopped

2 garlic cloves, finely chopped

3 tbsp olive oil

method

- Preheat the oven to 350°F/180°C/Gas Mark 4. Using a sharp knife, cut the bread into fancy shapes, such as half-moons, stars and Christmas trees. Drizzle with oil, transfer to an ovenproof dish and cook in the preheated oven for 15 minutes.
- While the bread is cooking, make the pesto. Put the basil, pine kernels and garlic into a small bowl. Pour in the olive oil and stir together well.
- Remove the bread shapes from the oven and leave to cool. Spread a layer of pesto on the shapes, top each one with a piece of mozzarella and some caviar and serve.

gravadlax with cream cheese

 serves 6   20 minutes + 48 hours marinating   0 minutes

ingredients

500 g/1lb 2 oz salmon fillet, skin removed

2 tbsp sea salt

1 tbsp caster sugar

2 tbsp chopped fresh dill

pepper

1 tbsp chopped fresh tarragon

1 tsp Dijon mustard

juice of 1 lemon

TOPPING

400 g/14 oz cream cheese

1 tbsp chopped fresh chives

pinch of paprika

sprigs of fresh dill, to garnish

method

- Put the salmon into a shallow glass dish. Combine the sea salt, sugar and dill, then rub the mixture into the fish until well coated. Season with plenty of pepper. Cover with clingfilm and refrigerate for at least 48 hours, turning the salmon once.

- When ready to serve, put the chopped tarragon into a mixing bowl with the mustard and lemon juice. Season well. Remove the salmon from the refrigerator, chop into small pieces then add to the bowl. Stir until the salmon is well coated.

- To make the topping, put the cream cheese, chives and paprika into a separate bowl and mix well. Place a 10-cm/4-inch steel cooking ring or round biscuit cutter on each of 4 small serving plates. Divide the salmon between the four steel rings so that each ring is half-full. Level the surface of each one, then top with the cream cheese mixture. Smooth the surfaces, then carefully remove the steel rings. Garnish with sprigs of fresh dill and serve.

stilton & parsnip tartlets

 serves 4   20 minutes + 45 minutes to chill   25 – 30 minutes

ingredients

125 g/4¹/₂ oz plain flour, plus extra for
    dusting
pinch of salt
90 g/3¹/₄ oz butter
1 egg yolk

FILLING

1 small parsnip, peeled and cut into
    1 cm/¹/₂ inch pieces
1 stick celery, trimmed and cut into
    1 cm/¹/₂ inch pieces
1 whole egg
2 egg yolks
100 ml/3¹/₂ fl oz double cream
salt and freshly ground black pepper
85 g/3 oz Stilton cheese, crumbled

method

- Sift the flour and salt together in a bowl. Rub in the butter, then mix in the egg yolk to make a dough, adding a little cold water if needed. Roll out the pastry on a lightly floured surface and use to line four 9 cm/3¹/₂ inch tartlet tins. Chill in the refrigerator for 45 minutes.

- Preheat the oven to 400°F/200°C/Gas Mark 6. Line the tartlet cases with foil and baking beans and bake in the centre of the oven for 10 minutes. Remove the beans and foil and cook for a further 5 minutes.

- Blanch the vegetables in boiling water for 2 minutes, cool under cold water and dry on kitchen paper. Beat the egg and egg yolks together, add the cream and season well. Divide the vegetables and the cheese between the tartlet cases and pour over the egg mixture. Bake for 10-15 minutes until the tartlets are cooked and golden brown on top. Serve warm.

chicken liver pâté

 serves 4 – 6   8 minutes + cooling and chilling   20 minutes

ingredients

200 g/7 oz butter

225 g/8 oz trimmed chicken livers,
    thawed if frozen

2 tbsp Marsala or brandy

1$\frac{1}{2}$ tsp chopped fresh sage

1 garlic clove, coarsely chopped

150 ml/$\frac{1}{4}$ pint double cream

salt and pepper

fresh bay leaves or sage leaves,
    to garnish

Melba toast, to serve

method

- Melt 40 g/1$\frac{1}{2}$ oz of the butter in a large, heavy-based frying pan. Add the chicken livers and cook over a medium heat for about 4 minutes on each side. They should be browned on the outside but still pink in the middle. Transfer to a food processor and process until finely chopped.

- Stir the Marsala or brandy into the pan, scraping up any sediment with a wooden spoon, then add to the food processor with the chopped sage, garlic and 100 g/3$\frac{1}{2}$ oz of the remaining butter. Process until smooth. Add the cream, season with salt and pepper and process until thoroughly combined and smooth. Spoon the pâté into a dish or individual ramekins, smooth the surface and leave to cool completely.

- Melt the remaining butter, then spoon it over the surface of the pâté. Decorate with herb leaves, cool, then chill in the refrigerator. Serve with Melba toast.

festive prawn cocktail

 serves 8   30 minutes   0 minutes

ingredients

350 ml/12 fl oz mayonnaise

125 ml/4 fl oz tomato ketchup

1 tsp chilli sauce

1 tsp Worcestershire sauce

1 kg/2 lb 4 oz cooked tiger prawns

2 ruby grapefruits

lettuce leaves, shredded

2 avocados, peeled, stoned and diced

lime slices and dill sprigs, to garnish

method

- Mix together the mayonnaise, tomato ketchup, chilli sauce and Worcestershire sauce in a small bowl. Cover with clingfilm and place in the refrigerator until required.

- Remove the heads from the prawns and peel off the shells, leaving the tails intact. Slit along the length of the back of each prawn with a sharp knife and remove the dark vein. Cut off a slice from the top and bottom of each grapefruit, then peel off the skin and all the white pith. Cut between the membranes to separate the segments.

- When ready to serve, make a bed of shredded lettuce in the base of 8 glass dishes. Divide the prawns, grapefruit segments and avocados among them and spoon over the mayonnaise dressing. Serve garnished with lime slices and dill sprigs.

main courses

roast turkey with bread sauce

 serves 8   20 minutes   3¹/₂ hours

ingredients

1 quantity Chestnut and Sausage Stuffing
  (see page 58)
1 x 5-kg/11-lb turkey
55 g/2 oz butter
5 tbsp red wine
400 ml/14 fl oz chicken stock, bought
  fresh or made with a stock cube
1 tbsp cornflour
1 tsp French mustard
1 tsp sherry vinegar

BREAD SAUCE
1 onion, peeled
4 cloves
600 ml/1 pint milk
115 g/4 oz fresh white breadcrumbs
55 g/2 oz butter
salt and pepper

method

- Preheat the oven to 425°F/220°C/Gas Mark 7. Spoon the stuffing into the neck cavity of the turkey and close the flap of skin with a skewer. Place the bird in a large roasting tin and rub all over with 40 g/1¹/₂ oz of the butter. Roast for 1 hour, then lower the oven temperature to 350°F/180°C/Gas Mark 4 and roast for a further 2¹/₂ hours. You may need to pour off the fat from the roasting tin occasionally.

- Meanwhile, make the bread sauce. Stud the onion with the cloves, then place in a saucepan with the milk, breadcrumbs and butter. Bring just to boiling point over a low heat, then remove from the heat and leave to stand in a warm place to infuse. Just before serving, remove the onion and reheat the sauce gently, beating well with a wooden spoon. Season to taste with salt and pepper.

- Check that the turkey is cooked by inserting a skewer or the point of a sharp knife into the thigh; if the juices run clear, it is ready. Transfer the bird to a carving board, cover loosely with foil and leave to rest.

- To make the gravy, skim off the fat from the roasting tin then place the tin over a medium heat. Add the red wine and stir with a wooden spoon, scraping up the sediment from the base of the tin. Stir in the chicken stock. Mix the cornflour, mustard, vinegar and 2 teaspoons water together in a small bowl, then stir into the wine and stock. Bring to the boil, stirring constantly until thickened and smooth. Stir in the remaining butter.

- Carve the turkey and serve with the warm bread sauce and all the trimmings - including stuffing, potatoes and gravy.

yuletide goose
with honey & pears

 serves 4 - 6   20 minutes   3 – 3$^1/_2$ hours

ingredients

3.5-4.5 kg/7$^3/_4$-10 lb oven-ready goose

1 tsp salt

4 pears

1 tbsp lemon juice

4 tbsp butter

2 tbsp honey

lemon slices, to garnish

TO SERVE

Perfect Roast Potatoes (see page 46)

Spiced Winter Vegetables (see page 54)

Brussels Sprouts with Buttered
    Chestnuts (see page 48)

Honey-Glazed Red Cabbage with
    Sultanas (see page 52)

method

- Preheat the oven to 425°F/220°C/Gas Mark 7. Rinse the goose and pat dry. Use a fork to prick the skin all over, then rub with salt. Place the bird upside down on a rack in a roasting tin. Roast for 30 minutes. Drain off the fat. Turn the bird over and roast for 15 minutes. Drain off the fat. Reduce the heat to 350°F/180°C/Gas Mark 4 and roast for 15 minutes per 450 g/1 lb. Cover with foil 15 minutes before the end of the cooking time. Check that the bird is cooked by inserting a knife between the legs and body. If the juices run clear, it is cooked. Remove from the oven.

- Peel and halve the pears and brush with lemon juice. Melt the butter and honey in a pan over a low heat, then add the pears. Cook, stirring, for 5-10 minutes, until tender. Remove from the heat, arrange the pears around the goose and pour the sweet juices over the bird. Garnish with lemon slices and serve with roast potatoes, winter vegetables, Brussels sprouts and red cabbage.

glazed ham

 serves 8   20 minutes   4¹/₄ hours

ingredients

1 x 4-kg/9-lb gammon joint

1 apple, cored and chopped

1 onion, chopped

300 ml/¹/₂ pint cider

6 black peppercorns

1 bouquet garni

bay leaf

about 50 cloves

4 tbsp demerara sugar

method

- Put the gammon in a large saucepan and add enough cold water to cover. Bring to the boil and skim off the scum that rises to the surface. Reduce the heat and simmer for 30 minutes. Drain the gammon and return to the saucepan. Add the apple, onion, cider, peppercorns, bouquet garni, bay leaf and a few of the cloves. Pour in enough fresh water to cover and bring back to the boil. Cover and simmer for 3 hours 20 minutes.

- Preheat the oven to 400°F/200°C/Gas Mark 6. Take the saucepan off the heat and set aside to cool slightly. Remove the gammon from the cooking liquid and, while it is still warm, loosen the rind with a sharp knife, then peel it off and discard. Score the fat into diamond shapes and stud with the remaining cloves. Place the gammon on a rack in a roasting tin and sprinkle with the sugar. Roast, basting occasionally with the cooking liquid, for 20 minutes. Serve hot, or cold later.

sliced duck breast with
madeira & blueberries

 serves 4   15 minutes + 1 hour marinating   15 minutes

ingredients

4 duck breasts (skin left on)
4 garlic clove, chopped
grated rind and juice of 1 orange
1 tbsp chopped fresh parsley
salt and pepper

MADEIRA & BLUEBERRY SAUCE
150 g/5½ oz blueberries
250 ml/9 fl oz Madeira
1 tbsp redcurrant jelly
blueberries and orange slices, to garnish
new potatoes and a selection of freshly
  cooked vegetables, to serve

method

- Use a sharp knife to make several shallow diagonal cuts in each duck breast. Put the duck in a glass bowl with the garlic, orange and parsley. Season, and stir well. Turn the duck in the mixture until thoroughly coated. Cover with clingfilm and leave in the refrigerator to marinate for at least 1 hour.
- Heat a dry, non-stick frying pan over a medium heat. Add the duck breasts and cook for 4 minutes, then turn them over and cook for a further 4 minutes or according to taste. Remove from the heat, cover the pan, and leave to stand for 5 minutes.
- Halfway through the cooking time, put the blueberries, Madeira and redcurrant jelly into a separate pan. Bring to the boil. Reduce the heat and simmer for 10 minutes, then remove from the heat.
- Slice the duck breasts and transfer to serving plates. Serve with the sauce poured over and accompanied by new potatoes and a selection of green vegetables.

roast pheasant with
red wine & herbs

 serves 4   20 minutes   1 hour

ingredients

100 g/3½ oz butter, slightly softened

1 tbsp chopped fresh thyme

1 tbsp chopped fresh parsley

2 oven-ready young pheasants

salt and pepper

4 tbsp vegetable oil

125 ml/4 fl oz red wine

Good quality, hand-fried crisps
(traditionally know as Game Chips) and
    freshly cooked vegetables, to serve

method

- Preheat the oven to 375°F/190°C/Gas Mark 5. Put the butter into a small bowl and mix in the chopped herbs. Lift the skins off the pheasants, taking care not to tear them, and push the herb butter under the skins. Season with salt and pepper. Pour the oil into a roasting tin, add the pheasants and cook in the preheated oven for 45 minutes, basting occasionally. Remove from the oven, pour over the red wine, then return to the oven and cook for another 15 minutes, or until cooked through. Check that each bird is cooked by inserting a knife between the legs and body. If the juices run clear, they are cooked.

- Remove the pheasants from the oven, cover with foil and leave to stand for 15 minutes. Serve garnished with game chips. Cut the pheasants into portions and accompany with seasonal vegetables.

festive beef wellington

 serves 4   20 minutes   1 hour 10 minutes

ingredients

750 g/1 lb 10 oz thick beef fillet

2 tbsp butter

salt and pepper

2 tbsp vegetable oil

1 garlic clove, chopped

1 onion, chopped

175 g/6 oz chestnut mushrooms

1 tbsp chopped fresh sage

salt and pepper

350 g/12 oz frozen puff pastry, defrosted

1 egg, beaten

chopped fresh sage, to garnish

seasonal vegetables, to serve

method

- Preheat the oven to 425°F/220°C/Gas Mark 7. Put the beef in a roasting tin, spread with butter and season. Roast for 30 minutes, then remove from the oven. Meanwhile, heat the oil in a pan over a medium heat. Add the garlic and onion and cook, stirring, for 3 minutes. Stir in the mushrooms, sage and seasoning and cook for 5 minutes. Remove from the heat.

- Roll out the pastry into a rectangle large enough to enclose the beef, then place the beef in the middle and spread the mushroom mixture over it. Bring the long sides of the pastry together over the beef and seal with beaten egg. Tuck the short ends over (trim away excess pastry) and seal. Place on a baking sheet, seam-side down. Make 2 slits in the top. Decorate with dough shapes and brush with beaten egg. Bake for 40 minutes. If the pastry browns too quickly, cover with foil. Remove from the oven and cut into thick slices. Serve with seasonal vegetables.

herbed salmon

with hollandaise sauce

 serves 4   15 minutes   8 - 10 minutes

ingredients

4 salmon fillets, about 175 g/6 oz each,
    skin removed

salt and pepper

2 tbsp olive oil

1 tbsp chopped fresh dill

1 tbsp chopped fresh chives

HOLLANDAISE SAUCE

3 egg yolks

1 tbsp water

salt and pepper

225 g/8 oz butter, cut into small cubes

juice of 1 lemon

chopped fresh chives, to garnish

new potatoes, sprouting broccoli and
    sesame seeds, to serve

method

- Preheat the grill to medium. Rinse the fish fillets under cold running water and pat dry with kitchen paper. Season with salt and pepper. Combine the olive oil with the dill and chives, then brush the mixture over the fish. Transfer to the grill and cook for about 6-8 minutes, turning once and brushing with more oil and herb mixture, until cooked to your taste.

- Meanwhile, to make the sauce, put the egg yolks in a heatproof bowl over a pan of boiling water (or use a double boiler). Add the water and season with salt and pepper. Lower the heat and simmer, whisking constantly, until the mixture begins to thicken. Whisk in the butter, cube by cube, until the mixture is thick and shiny. Whisk in the lemon juice, then remove from the heat.

- Remove the fish from the grill and transfer to individual serving plates. Pour over the sauce and garnish with chopped fresh chives. Serve with new potatoes and sprouting broccoli garnished with sesame seeds.

mixed nut roast with

cranberry & red wine sauce

 serves 4   30 minutes   35 minutes

ingredients

2 tbsp butter, plus extra for greasing

2 garlic cloves, chopped

1 large onion, chopped

50 g/1³⁄₄ oz pine kernels, toasted

75 g/2³⁄₄ oz hazelnuts, toasted

50 g/1³⁄₄ oz walnuts, ground

50 g/1³⁄₄ oz cashew nuts, ground

100 g/3¹⁄₂ oz wholemeal breadcrumbs

1 egg, lightly beaten

2 tbsp chopped fresh thyme

250 ml/9 fl oz vegetable stock

salt and pepper

sprigs of fresh thyme, to garnish

Brussels sprouts with toasted
    almonds, to serve

CRANBERRY & RED WINE SAUCE

175 g/6 oz fresh cranberries

100 g/3¹⁄₂ oz caster sugar

300 ml/10 fl oz red wine

1 cinnamon stick

method

● Preheat the oven to 350°F/180°C/Gas Mark 4. Grease a loaf tin and line it with greaseproof paper. Melt the butter in a saucepan over a medium heat. Add the garlic and onion and cook, stirring, for about 3 minutes. Remove the pan from the heat. Grind the pine kernels and hazelnuts. Stir all the nuts into the pan and add the breadcrumbs, egg, thyme, stock and seasoning.

● Spoon the mixture into the loaf tin and level the surface. Cook in the centre of the preheated oven for 30 minutes or until cooked through and golden. The loaf is cooked when a skewer inserted into the centre comes out clean. Halfway through the cooking time, make the sauce. Put all the ingredients in a saucepan and bring to the boil. Reduce the heat and simmer, stirring occasionally, for 15 minutes.

● To serve, remove the sauce from the heat and discard the cinnamon stick. Remove the nut roast from the oven and turn out. Garnish with thyme; serve with the sauce and Brussels sprouts.

feta cheese & cranberry tarts

 serves 4   20 minutes   15 minutes

ingredients

4 tbsp olive oil

1 onion, chopped

8 black olives, stoned and chopped

85 g/3 oz cranberries

1 eating apple

1 tbsp lemon juice

8 sheets of filo pastry, cut into 16 squares
measuring 13 cm/5 inches across

125 g/4½ oz feta cheese, cut into small cubes

method

- Preheat the oven to 350°F/180°C/Gas Mark 4. Heat 2 tablespoons of oil in a frying pan over a medium heat. Add the onion and cook, stirring, for 3 minutes, until slightly softened. Remove from the heat and stir in the olives and cranberries. Core and chop the apple and add it to the pan with the lemon juice. Stir well and set aside.

- Brush the filo squares with the remaining oil and use them to line 4 small flan tins. Place 4 sheets in each tin, staggering them so that the overhanging corners make a decorative star shape.

- Divide the cranberry filling between the four pastry cases. Scatter over the feta cheese and bake in the centre of the preheated oven for about 10 minutes until golden. Serve warm.

vegetables & side dishes

perfect roast potatoes

 serves 8   10 minutes   1 hour 25 minutes

ingredients

70 g/2¹/₂ oz goose fat or duck fat or
    5 tbsp olive oil
coarse sea salt
1 kg/2 lb 4 oz even-sized potatoes, peeled
8 fresh rosemary sprigs, to garnish

method

- Preheat the oven to 450°F/230°C/Gas Mark 9. Put the fat or oil in a large roasting tin, sprinkle generously with sea salt and place in the oven.

- Meanwhile, cook the potatoes in a large pan of boiling water for 8-10 minutes, until parboiled. Drain well, and if the potatoes are large, cut them in half. Return the potatoes to the pan and shake vigorously to roughen their outsides.

- Arrange the potatoes in a single layer in the hot tin and roast for 45 minutes. If they look as if they are beginning to char around the edges, lower the oven temperature to 200°C/400°F/Gas Mark 6. Turn the potatoes over and roast for a further 30 minutes, until crisp. Serve garnished with sprigs of rosemary.

brussels sprouts

with buttered chestnuts

 serves 4   10 minutes   10 minutes

ingredients

350 g/12 oz Brussels sprouts, trimmed

3 tbsp butter

100 g/3½ oz canned whole chestnuts

pinch of nutmeg

salt and pepper

50 g/1¾ oz flaked almonds, to garnish

method

- Bring a large saucepan of salted water to the boil. Add the Brussels sprouts and cook for 5 minutes. Drain thoroughly.
- Melt the butter in a large saucepan over a medium heat. Add the Brussels sprouts and cook, stirring, for 3 minutes, then add the chestnuts and nutmeg. Season with salt and pepper and stir well. Cook for another 2 minutes, stirring, then remove from the heat. Transfer to a serving dish, scatter over the almonds and serve.

glazed parsnips

 serves 8   10 minutes   35 – 45 minutes

ingredients

24 small parsnips, peeled

about 1 tsp salt

115 g/4 oz butter

115 g/3 oz soft brown sugar

method

- Place the parsnips in a saucepan, add just enough water to cover then add the salt. Bring to the boil, reduce the heat, cover, and simmer for 20-25 minutes, until tender. Drain well.
- Melt the butter in a heavy pan or wok. Add the parsnips and toss well. Sprinkle with the sugar then cook, stirring frequently to prevent the sugar from sticking to the pan or burning. Cook the parsnips for 10-15 minutes, until golden and glazed. Transfer to a warm serving dish and serve immediately.

honey-glazed red cabbage
with sultanas

 serves 4   10 minutes   50 minutes

ingredients

2 tbsp butter

1 garlic clove, chopped

650 g/1 lb 7 oz red cabbage, shredded

150 g/5½ oz sultanas

1 tbsp honey

100 ml/3½ fl oz red wine

100 ml/3½ fl oz water

method

- Melt the butter in a large saucepan over a medium heat. Add the garlic and cook, stirring, for 1 minute, until slightly softened.
- Add the cabbage and sultanas, then stir in the honey. Cook for another minute. Pour in the wine and water and bring to the boil. Reduce the heat, cover and simmer, stirring occasionally, for about 45 minutes or until the cabbage is cooked. Serve hot.

spiced winter vegetables

 serves 4   15 minutes   1 hour 10 minutes

ingredients

4 parsnips, scrubbed and trimmed but left
   unpeeled

4 carrots, scrubbed and trimmed but left
   unpeeled

2 onions, quartered

1 red onion, quartered

3 leeks, trimmed and cut into 6 cm/
   2$^{1}/_{2}$ inch slices

6 cloves of garlic, left unpeeled and whole

6 tbsp extra-virgin olive oil

$^{1}/_{2}$ tsp mild chilli powder

pinch of paprika

salt and freshly ground black pepper

method

● Preheat the oven to 425°F/220°C/Gas Mark 7. Bring a large saucepan of water to the boil.

● Cut the parsnips and carrots into wedges of similar size. Add them to the pan and cook for 5 minutes. Drain thoroughly and place in an ovenproof dish with the onions, leeks and garlic. Pour over the olive oil, sprinkle in the spices and mix until all the vegetables are well coated.

● Roast in the preheated oven for at least 1 hour. Turn the vegetables from time to time until they are tender and starting to colour. Remove from the oven, transfer to a serving dish and serve.

garlic mushrooms with
white wine & chestnuts

 serves 4   15 minutes   10 minutes

ingredients

4 tbsp butter

4 garlic cloves, chopped

200 g/7 oz button mushrooms, sliced

200 g/7 oz chestnut mushrooms, sliced

4 tbsp dry white wine

100 ml/3½ fl oz double cream

salt and pepper

300 g/10½ oz canned whole chestnuts

100 g/3½ oz chanterelle mushrooms, sliced

chopped fresh parsley, to garnish

method

- Melt the butter in a large saucepan over a medium heat. Add the garlic and cook, stirring, for 3 minutes, until softened. Add the button and chestnut mushrooms and cook for another 3 minutes.

- Stir in the wine and cream and season with salt and pepper. Cook for 2 minutes, stirring, then add the chestnuts and the chanterelle mushrooms. Cook for another 2 minutes, stirring, then remove from the heat and transfer to a serving dish. Garnish with chopped fresh parsley and serve.

chestnut and sausage stuffing

 serves 6 – 8   15 minutes   30 – 40 minutes

ingredients

225 g/8 oz pork sausagemeat

225 g/8 oz unsweetened
    chestnut purée

85 g/3 oz walnuts, chopped

115 g/4 oz ready-to-eat dried apricots,
    chopped

2 tbsp chopped fresh parsley

2 tbsp chopped fresh chives

2 tsp chopped fresh sage

4-5 tbsp double cream

salt and pepper

method

- Combine the sausagemeat and chestnut purée in a bowl, then stir in the walnuts, apricots, parsley, chives and sage. Stir in enough double cream to make a firm, but not dry, mixture. Season with salt and pepper.

- If you are planning to stuff a turkey or goose, fill only the neck cavity. It is safer and more reliable to cook the stuffing separately, either rolled into small balls and placed on a baking sheet, or spooned into an ovenproof dish.

- Cook the separate stuffing in an oven for 30-40 minutes at 375°F/190°C/Gas Mark 5. It should be allowed a longer time if you are roasting a bird at a lower temperature in the same oven.

cranberry sauce

 serves 8   10 minutes   10 – 12 minutes

ingredients

thinly pared rind and juice
    of 1 lemon
thinly pared rind and juice
    of 1 orange
350 g/12 oz cranberries, thawed if frozen
140 g/5 oz caster sugar
2 tbsp arrowroot mixed with
    3 tbsp cold water

method

- Cut strips of lemon and orange rind into thin shreds and place in a heavy-based saucepan. If using fresh cranberries, rinse well and remove any stalks. Add the berries, citrus juice and sugar and cook over a medium heat, stirring occasionally, for about 5 minutes, until the berries begin to burst.

- Strain the juice into a clean saucepan and reserve the cranberries. Stir the arrowroot mixture into the juice, then bring to the boil, stirring constantly, until the sauce is smooth and thickened. Remove from the heat and stir in the reserved cranberries.

- Transfer the cranberry sauce to a bowl for serving. Serve warm or cold.

desserts, sweets & drinks

christmas pudding

 serves 10 - 12   2$\frac{1}{4}$ hours + 2 – 8 weeks chilling   8 hours

ingredients

200 g/7 oz currants

200 g/7 oz raisins

200 g/7 oz sultanas

150 ml/5 fl oz sweet sherry

175 g/6 oz butter, plus extra
   for greasing

175 g/6 oz brown sugar

4 eggs, beaten

150 g/5$\frac{1}{2}$ oz self-raising flour

100 g/3$\frac{1}{2}$ oz fresh white or
   wholemeal breadcrumbs

50 g/1$\frac{3}{4}$ oz blanched almonds, chopped

juice of 1 orange

grated rind of $\frac{1}{2}$ orange

grated rind of $\frac{1}{2}$ lemon

$\frac{1}{2}$ tsp ground mixed spice

holly leaves and icing sugar to decorate

method

- Put the currants, raisins and sultanas into a glass bowl and pour over the sherry. Leave to soak for at least 2 hours.

- Mix the butter and sugar in a bowl. Beat in the eggs, then fold in the flour. Stir in the soaked fruit and sherry with the breadcrumbs, almonds, orange juice and rind, lemon rind and mixed spice. Grease a pudding basin and press the mixture into it, leaving a gap of 2.5 cm/1 inch at the top. Cut a circle of greaseproof paper 3 cm/1$\frac{1}{4}$ inches larger than the top of the basin, grease with butter and place over the pudding. Secure with string, then top with 2 layers of foil. Place the pudding in a pan filled with boiling water which reaches two-thirds of the way up the basin. Reduce the heat and simmer for 6 hours, topping up the water when necessary.

- Remove from the heat and leave to cool. Renew the greaseproof paper and foil and refrigerate for 2-8 weeks. To reheat, steam for 2 hours as before. Decorate with holly and a sprinkling of icing sugar.

festive mince pies

 Makes 12 – 16   20 minutes   15 minutes

ingredients

200 g/7 oz plain flour, plus extra
   for dusting

100 g/3$^1\!/_2$ oz butter

25 g/1 oz icing sugar

1 egg yolk

2-3 tbsp milk

milk for glazing

300 g/10$^1\!/_3$ oz mincemeat

icing sugar, for dusting

sprigs of holly, to decorate

method

● Preheat the oven to 350°F/180°C/Gas Mark 4. Sift the flour into a mixing bowl. Using your fingertips, rub in the butter until the mixture resembles breadcrumbs. Mix in the sugar and egg yolk. Stir in enough milk to make a soft dough, turn out onto a lightly floured work surface and knead lightly until smooth.

● Shape the dough into a ball and roll out to a thickness of 1 cm/$^1\!/_2$ inch. Use fluted cutters to cut out 16 rounds of 7 cm/2$^1\!/_2$ inches diameter and use to line greased tartlet tins. Half fill each pie with mincemeat. Cut out 16 star shapes, brush them with milk and place on top of each pie. Glaze the surface with more milk and bake in the oven for 15 minutes until the pastry is a pale golden colour. Remove from the oven and cool on a wire rack. Dust with icing sugar before serving.

christmas cake

 makes one 20-cm/8-inch cake   45 minutes + 8 hours soaking   3 hours

ingredients

150 g/5^1/$_2$ oz raisins

125 g/4^1/$_2$ oz stoned dates, chopped

125 g/4^1/$_2$ oz sultanas

100 g/3^1/$_2$ oz glacé cherries, rinsed

150 ml/5 fl oz brandy

225 g/8 oz butter, plus extra
    for greasing

200 g/7 oz caster sugar

4 eggs

grated rind of 1 orange and 1 lemon

1 tbsp black treacle

225 g/8 oz plain flour

^{1}/$_2$ tsp salt

^{1}/$_2$ tsp baking powder

1 tsp mixed spice

25 g/1 oz toasted almonds, chopped

25 g/1 oz toasted hazelnuts, chopped

750 g/1 lb 10 oz marzipan

3 tbsp apricot jam

3 egg whites

650 g/1 lb 7 oz icing sugar

method

- Make this cake at least 3 weeks in advance. Put all the fruit in a bowl, pour over the brandy and soak overnight.

- Preheat the oven to 225°F/110°C/Gas Mark ^{1}/$_4$. Grease a 20-cm/ 8-inch cake tin and line it with greaseproof paper. In a bowl, cream together the butter and sugar until fluffy. Gradually beat in the eggs. Stir in the citrus rind and black treacle. In a separate bowl, sift together the flour, salt, baking powder and mixed spice, then fold into the egg mixture. Fold in the fruit, brandy and nuts, then spoon into the cake tin. Bake for at least 3 hours. If it browns too quickly, cover with foil. The cake is cooked when a skewer inserted into the centre comes out clean. Remove from the oven and cool on a wire rack. Store in an airtight container until required.

- Roll out the marzipan and cut to shape to cover the top and sides of the cake. Brush the cake with the jam and press the marzipan onto the surface. Make the icing by placing the egg whites in a mixing bowl and add the icing sugar a little at a time, beating well until the icing is very thick and will stand up in peaks. Then spread over the covered cake, using a fork to give texture. Decorate as you wish with silver dragées and ribbon.

yule log

 serves 8   35 minutes + frosting and decorating   15 minutes

ingredients

butter, for greasing

115 g/4 oz self-raising flour,
     plus extra for dusting

150 g/5 oz caster sugar, plus extra for
     sprinkling

4 eggs, separated

1 tsp almond essence

280 g/10 oz plain chocolate, broken into
     squares

225 ml/8 fl oz double cream

2 tbsp rum

holly, to decorate

icing sugar, for dusting

method

- Preheat the oven to 375°F/190°C/Gas Mark 5. Grease and line a 40 x 28-cm/16 x 11-inch Swiss roll tin and dust with flour.
- Reserve 2 tablespoons of the sugar and whisk the remainder with the egg yolks until thick and pale. Stir in the almond essence. Whisk the egg white in a clean, grease-free bowl until soft peaks form. Gradually whisk in the reserved sugar until stiff and glossy. Sift half the flour over the egg yolk mixture and fold in, then fold in one-quarter of the egg whites. Sift and fold in the remaining flour, followed by the remaining egg whites. Spoon the mixture into the tin, spreading it out evenly with a palette knife. Bake for about 15 minutes, until light golden.
- Sprinkle caster sugar over a sheet of greaseproof paper and turn out the cake onto the paper. Roll up and leave to cool.
- Place the chocolate in a heatproof bowl. Bring the cream to boiling point in a small saucepan, then pour over the chocolate and stir until it has melted. Beat with an electric mixer until smooth and thick. Reserve about one-third of the chocolate mixture and stir the rum into the remainder.
- Unroll the cake and spread the chocolate and rum mixture over it. Reroll and place on a plate or silver board. Spread the reserved chocolate mixture evenly over the top and sides. Mark with a fork so that the surface resembles tree bark. Just before serving, decorate with holly and a sprinkling of icing sugar.

festive sherry trifle

 serves 4 - 6   15 minutes + 6 hours soaking/chilling   2 – 3 minutes

ingredients

100 g/3½ oz trifle sponges

150 ml/5 fl oz raspberry jam

150 ml/5 fl oz sherry

150 g/5½ oz frozen raspberries,

350 g/12 oz fresh strawberries, sliced

CUSTARD LAYER

6 egg yolks

50 g/1¾ oz caster sugar

500 ml/18 fl oz milk

1 tsp vanilla essence

TOPPING

300 ml/10 fl oz double cream

1-2 tbsp caster sugar

1 chocolate flake, crumbled

method

- Spread the trifle sponges with jam, cut them into bite-sized cubes and arrange in the bottom of a large glass serving bowl. Pour over the sherry and leave for 30 minutes.

- Mix together the raspberries and strawberries and spoon over the sponge.

- To make the custard, put the egg yolks and sugar into a bowl and whisk together. Pour the milk into a pan and warm gently over a low heat. Remove from the heat and gradually stir into the egg mixture, then return the mixture to the pan and stir constantly over a low heat until thickened. Do not boil. Remove from the heat, pour into a bowl and stir in the vanilla. Cool for 1 hour. Spread the custard over the trifle, cover with clingfilm and chill for 2 hours.

- To make the topping, whip the cream in a bowl and stir in sugar to taste. Spread over the trifle, and then scatter over the chocolate flake pieces. Chill for ½ an hour before serving.

white chocolate truffles

 makes 20   15 minutes + 2$\frac{1}{2}$ − 3 hours chilling   5 minutes

ingredients

120 g/4$\frac{1}{4}$ oz white chocolate, broken into
   small, even-sized pieces
4 tbsp butter, softened to room
   temperature
2 tbsp double cream
$\frac{1}{2}$ tsp brandy
grated white chocolate, to decorate

method

- Put the chocolate pieces into a heatproof glass bowl and place over a pan of hot but not simmering water. When it starts to melt, stir gently until completely melted. Do not overheat, or the chocolate will separate. Remove from the heat and gently stir in the butter, then the cream and brandy. Leave to cool, then cover with clingfilm and refrigerate for 2–2 $\frac{1}{2}$ hours until set.

- Remove the chocolate mixture from the refrigerator. Using a teaspoon, scoop out small pieces of the mixture, then use your hands to roll them into balls. To decorate, roll the balls in grated white chocolate. To store, transfer to an airtight container and refrigerate for up to 12 days.

mulled wine

 serves 4   5 – 10 minutes   5 – 10 minutes

ingredients

750 ml/1⅓ pints of red wine

3 tbsp sherry

8 cloves

1 cinnamon stick

½ tsp ground mixed spice

2 tbsp clear honey

1 seedless orange, cut into wedges

1 lemon, cut into wedges

method

- Put the wine, sherry, cloves, cinnamon, mixed spice and honey into a saucepan and stir together well. Warm over a low heat, stirring, until just starting to simmer, but do not let it boil. Remove from the heat and strain through a sieve. Discard the cloves and cinnamon stick.

- Return the wine to the pan with the orange and lemon wedges. Warm gently over a very low heat, but do not let it boil. Remove from the heat, pour into heatproof glasses and serve hot.

hot rum punch

 serves 10   15 minutes   0 minutes

ingredients

850 ml/1$\frac{1}{2}$ pints rum

850 ml/1$\frac{1}{2}$ pints brandy

600 ml/1 pint freshly squeezed lemon juice

3-4 tbsp caster sugar

2 litres/3$\frac{1}{2}$ pints boiling water

orange and lemon slices,
    to decorate

method

• Mix together the rum, brandy, lemon juice and 3 tablespoons of the sugar in a punch bowl or large mixing bowl. Pour in the boiling water and stir well to mix. Taste and add more sugar if required. Decorate with the fruit slices and serve immediately in heatproof glasses.

index